HUDDLESTON FAMILY HISTORY

by Henry Stonewall Huddleston

Order this book online at www.trafford.com
or email orders@trafford.com

Most Trafford titles are also available at major online book retailers.

Note for Librarians: A cataloguing record for this book is available from Library and Archives Canada at www.collectionscanada.ca/amicus/index-e.html

Printed in Victoria, BC, Canada.

ISBN: 978-1-4269-1672-4 (sc)

Our mission is to efficiently provide the world's finest, most comprehensive book publishing service, enabling every author to experience success. To find out how to publish your book, your way, and have it available worldwide, visit us online at www.trafford.com

Trafford rev. 9/21/2009

www.trafford.com

North America & international
toll-free: 1 888 232 4444 (USA & Canada)
phone: 250 383 6864 ♦ fax: 812 355 4082

Family

PREFACE

I am Henry Stonewall Huddleston and am trying to learn to be a writer. This may be hopeless at eighty years old but I can remember my father saying "Quitters lose". One of my nephews Chuck Huddleston read part of my first attempt at a novel and was either being polite or he really liked it. At any rate he suggested I put all the stories about the family I could remember into book form. He didn't say, before I died, but I am sure that was in his mind. Some of the things I remember I won't tell.

I finished high school in Lebanon, Tennessee by passing a GED test in the Marine Corps. My mother accepted my diploma at the twelfth grade graduation for me as I happened to be a pot walloper on mess duty at Eva Marine Air Station, Oahu, Hawaii at the time.

I have been a sheet metal worker, a mechanical contractor, and from

Family

fifty years old until seventy I was president of Design Engineering Services Inc. in San Francisco, California. We did HVAC, plumbing. Piping and fire protection design work on projects from Maine to Hawaii and the Philippines. If that seems a little strange to you, It does to me also but we made it work. I had the invaluable help of a group of sterling people including Richard Ehrenberg, James Morel, Dave Penney, Diana T, Peter Skillman and of course the good right hand Mimi Rourke.

If you like my recitation about my screwy family please say so. If you don't, I don't want to hear it.

I also know that it is poor grammar composition to start and end sentences with a preposition. That's the way I talk.

Family

This is the year 2009 and I am eighty years old. Did I already say that?

The following is mostly from my memory and may have no relationship to any person living or dead and may have no reference to actual events.

I have been thinking about this for a while and decided there is a monumental amount of trivia no one would be much interested in so I will write something up and bore all my relatives to tears. They will feel obligated to read it. - - - I think.

Rumor has it that the original spelling of the family name was de Hodelson. The most common spelling now Is Huddleston although there are several variations such as Huttlestun, Huddlestun, Heddleston and god knows what else.

Somebody thought the name originated in Normandy and the first records were around the year 1066

Family

but they didn't write much in those days. Some time around then some of them emigrated to what we now call England and settled in an Yorkshire. There is an ancient village about ten miles east of Leeds named Huddleston, a house called Huddleston manor, still occupied by a farmer who "don't know nothing about it" and a wooded area called Huddleston wood.

The family apparently prospered and did well with substantial land ownership and many offspring including one who became Archbishop of Canterbury. Then they backed the wrong political party and things turned unhappy.

Several families emigrated to America and someone thinks we are descendants of Valentine who emigrated to Maryland about 1663. Possibly under clouded circumstances. Something to do with poaching on the king's preserves. Don't know exactly what presrves. He later moved to Newport Rhode Island where his two sons were born. Henry in

Family

1673, George in 1677 and Katherine (DOB Unknown).

The stories I heard when I was a Kid were that George and Henry under some circumstances or other went to West Virginia. There are some records of land ownership in that area. They later left West Virginia and George went to Indiana and married 9 that may be a polite term) believed to be an Indian woman (not Pocahontas).

HENRY went to central Tennessee and had numerous descendents. My name is Henry and I happen to be the eighth in line, not quite direct. I have always enjoyed being Henry the Eighth. How many wives did he kill?

My grandfather on my father's side who I believe was a descendent of some Huddlestons who emigrated to The Carolinas some time in the early seventeen hundreds. His name was Jack, they called him Wild Jack He lived in Davidson County Tennessee and had had several children as was usual in those

Family

days. Kids were cheaper than hiring help to run the farm since the damn yankees had stopped slavery. As I remember he had Walter Albert, my father, Henry, Allen (uncle Alley), Stonewall, Sally and maybe some others I don't remember.

JACK owned a fairly big farm and a general store in and around Carthage, Tennessee. His wife died when the youngest Kid was about 6 and he was running the farm and the general store with the kids.

Carthage is about 8 miles from Nashville and about every four or five months the pressure would get too much for him and he would go down to Nashville and tie one on. This particular night he was in a saloon and got into a disagreement with some gentlemen. Things progressed along to fisticuffs and Jack happened to have positioned himself near a stack of beer bottles. Being in an aggressive frame of mind he ran all the gentlemen out of the bar out by throwing beer

Family

bottles at them. Too bad he was too early for professional baseball.

A deputy sheriff became aware that there was another disturbance at that particular saloon. After consulting with the gentlemen out side the bar he stuck his head around the door. Jack delivered a beer bottle chest high and across the center of the plate striking the deputy between the eyes resulting in instant death. In those days a beer bottle had substantial weight.

This caused considerable consternation with the local law enforcement people and in due course Jack was arrested and placed in a cell on the second floor of the sheriff's office pending a trial tomorrow. Jack understood that justice in those days was try him today and hang him in the morning. Jury selection was grab twelve people off the street and lets get on with it. They did not understand about appeals etc.

7

Family

Jack was a rather muscular individual and it seemed to him that he was in an untenable position that most likely was going to have an unpleasant outcome. He, later that night pulled the bars off the window and jumped to the ground spraining his ankle in the process. He limped down to the Cumberland River that was nearby, swam the river and ended up in a black neighborhood. He met up with a black man, explained his problem and found a kindred soul. He as not heard from for Twelve years.

About twelve years later they got a letter from Jack asking if they were still looking for him. They answered that they thought not so he came back to Tennessee bringing two sons with him. He had married in Texas and that wife also died after giving birth to the two sons. There is also a story that he, at some time during the twelve years, made a trip to California. Took him six months on horseback, decided he didn't like the place and went back to Texas.

Family

He had several incidents after he got home but the one that got him was an incident at a hog killing. After being severely cut one hog got away. He put a butcher knife handle first in his back pocket and chased after him. He jumped a rail fence and slashed his arm including an artery. They found him bled out and dead with the hog also dead about twenty feet ahead of him.

It is unclear to me what happened to the store and farm but Sally later married a man named Jack Jones who ran a very successful farm. I believe that is the farm. Don't know how all that came about.

The two boys grew up and went to Oklahoma. One worked for The Hughes Tool Company delivering drill bits to the oil well drillers. He drove up to a well site with a new bit just as the well blew natural gas. The truck lit off the gas and killed him.

Family

The other had a job welding pipe-lines. He was down in a trench that caved in and killed him.

ALLEN (Uncle Alley) worked almost 40 years as a mechanic for the Louisville and Nashville Railroad and built houses on the side. He hired my brothers when he could to help with the houses. He married a woman named Myrah and they had no children.

When he died he left her 42 slum houses in Nashville. I saw some of them and if a California building inspector saw one of them he would instantly go into cardiac arrest. What do you mean an outhouse, no running water and no electricity, in the city limits?

The last time I saw aunt Myrah she would ask me about every 3 minutes, "Now who are you?"

When she died it took the lawyers over two years to settle the estate and my share of the inheritance was

Family

$276.00. I suspect the lawyer inherited considerably more.

HENRY married a woman who my family never talked about when I was around although I suspect they talked about her considerably.
They had two girls named Imola and Creola. Make of that what you will but I suspect a Cherokee influence. The last time I saw uncle Henry he was working for the state Of Tennessee doing something with traffic planning. Died soon after of tuberculosis.

STONEWALL Moved to Oklahoma and operated an Indian trading post at Cash, Oklahoma near the local Indian reservation. Only saw him once when I was about 6 years old and he told stories about selling to Indians and eating cooked dog with them just to be friendly. He also had a story about fishing in a creek and met up with a man. They had a nice conversation and each went his way. Shortly after that he met up with a posse. Luckily they knew him. The man he had a

nice conversation with was Pretty
Boy Floyd and the posse was looking
for him.

He had two sons that I know about
who ran a funeral parlor in Cash
for years until they sold out to a
conglomerate about 1995. I have no
information on them since then.

WALTER ALBERT my father, was born
Nov. 19 1885. I know very little
of his early life. Walter was a
farmer and a trader in mules and
cotton. There is a story that he
had a hog killing one year when he
killed and butchered 400 hogs. Had
every wagon and team in the whole
area hauling pork into Lebanon for
the railroad.

WALTER married GRACE VICTORIA
HUDDLESTON in February 1908. The
families all seemed to agree that
this was okay. Not clear on the
exact circumstances of that but it
worked out very well. This situation has caused me to get some
strange looks for about 70 years.
Someone will ask my mothers maiden

name. When I tell them they say
"No, no her maiden name, before she
married. Then they look at me sort
of funny.

The house they had then was a large
southern mansion style that still
exists on highway 231 about half
way between Lebanon and Murfr-
eesboro. It is now a bed and brea-
kfast. He later sold that place and
moved to Nashville to pursue his
trading business where he bought
mules in Tennessee, moved them to
Alabama, sold them and bought
cotton which he shipped to Memphis
and sold to agents for the northern
textile mills.

A kind of sad sidelight was that
the mules he sold to people in
Alabama were used to pull trolley
cars in coal mines. They blinded
them so they weren't afraid to go
down into the mines. There was
always a market for them since they
didn't live very long in that environment. Neither did the miners
but my dad didn't sell any miners.

Family

At some point he bought a cotton farm near Walter Hill Tennessee, moved there and started a herd of dairy cows. My first real memories are of an all hands operation, literally, twice a day milking 40 cows. 75 years later I still have a pretty good grip.

I remember my brother Ben tied a brick on a cows tail to keep her from switching him in the face while he was milking her. We found him lying unconscious in a pool of spilled milk. Guess the cow had a pretty strong tail.

The fall of 1929 the farmers in that area including my father had harvested their cotton and sent to Memphis and sell it for them. This happened just before the bank failures tipping off the economic crash of 1929. Walter was friendly with several of the cotton buyers having sold to them for years. One of them told him he could give three cents a pound today. Tomorrow he would be stopped from buying at any price.

Family

My Dad sent a telegram to the other farmers telling them what was happening and they wired back five words. "Don't sell at 3 cents."

Dad sold anyway and cashed the check for gold backed hard cash. Now he figured that if he went home they would probably lynch him so he stayed in Memphis. Two days later the bank run started and the banks all closed. Dad then went home and was a minor hero because he had hard cash. Not much but still real money.

We stayed on the farm for I think 5 years. We had a big old boxy car that went in the first year. I think it was 1932 the kids did not start school (I was too young) because it was already cold weather and they had no shoes.

Each year Dad would make a deal with the local black people to harvest the crops. I remember several negros digging potatoes and harvesting corn for one bag of every three bags they filled. This also worked for vegetables but they were not much interested in picking cotton because they couldn't eat it and there was no market for cotton. The food the blacks earned working for farmers plus anything they could catch was probably all they had to eat for several years.

I believe it was in 1934 that the farm was sold for taxes. I seem to remember the total tax bill was about $200.00.

We moved into a house near Baird's Mill Cross roads and my dad went to work for the WPA. The WPA was the Works Progress Administration sponsored by president Roosevelt as a part of the New Deal. The WPA did some pretty nice things like road repairs, armory buildings, parks, museums and other projects. This was the one of item of Roosevelt's New Deal that actually did some good. This put people to work and helped keep the country more or less alive. 1935 was looking pretty bleak and things

Family

were starting to fail again economically. The Roosevelt administration managed to stall things along for three years until Adolph Hitler decided to rule the world. World war two broke the depression and made several millionaires when a million dollars was a lot of money.

Walter contracted Parkinson's disease about 1936 and finally died in 1940. We had moved three times between 1934 and 1940. First to a house on highway 231 near Major school which I attended until the sixth grade. The house burned down on a Sunday morning I think in 1939. I was staying with uncle Ben, Aunt Evie and aunt Fannie that morning. Uncle Ben and I were out squirrel hunting when we heard the dinner bell ringing. Uncle Ben said, "We better get back, something has happened."

When we got down to the house on highway 231 there was nothing but ashes, five partly standing chim-

Family

neys and a bunch of people standing around.

By this time my father's illness had progressed to the point where he could not even stand up so he was sitting in a rocking chair in the yard. This was the chair they carried him out of the house sitting in and incidentally the one he had lived in for the last two years. He was convinced that if he went to bed he would die so he stayed in that chair twenty four hours a day.

The day of the fire several people came around and offered help. I remember one man said, "Walter, I got that old house down by Vine church. Ain't nobody using it. Why don't you go on and move in there."

Another man came and said, "I got a lot of old furniture down in the barn. Ain't much but at least you will have a stove and something to sleep on. If you want it I'll bring it on down there." Several people brought food, clothing bedding and a lot of things I probably have forgotten. No one said anything about payment.

The fire happened on Sunday morning. Sunday night we had a house, furniture, food and clothing. This was rural Tennessee in the thirties and early forties. I think some of that attitude still exists in the rural areas

I can remember my father saying, "They are helping the Russians. They ought to let them and the Germans kill each other."

I really believe it was not Parkinson disease that killed him. The depression broke him. He died in 1940.

MY BROTHERS AND SISTER

WAlTER WILLIAM (Dick)
DOB 04/25/1909,- Died ? ? . 1999.
When Dick graduated from high school he went to live with uncle Ben and worked as a horse shoe man. I believe they called that a far-

rier. God knows why. He also got a job working for the state at Cedars of Lebanon State Park, one of the WPA projects, until the war started, then he got a job at Vultee aircraft plant in Nashville. He had asthma all his life and was ineligible for the draft. When Vultee cut back near the end of the war he went back to the park, got promoted and worked as park superintendent until his retirement.

Dick Married Lorene Edwards (Boots) and they had one child, Janice Faye. I wrecked Dick's car the night she was born. I went to the hospital where he was waiting through a hard labor with Lorene and told him what happened. Ever see anyone turn instant white? Faye was never married and still owns the Dick Huddleston farm. A cousin Connie Jordan Nee Edwards Is the executor of Dicks estate. Faye lives with her aunt Mamie, Connie's mother.

I remember when I got Married in Kansas City Missouri and took my

Family

new wife Barbara to Tennessee to meet the family. Dick took us on a tour of the park in a jeep. We were driving along a fire break road when he sniffed the air and suddenly stopped. He got out of the jeep and went off into the woods. Pretty soon he came back and grinning said, "Bring your new wife over here and let her see some real Tennessee."

We went into the woods and found a small creek with a whiskey still in full operation. There were about six 55 gallon drums full of something with the surface covered with dead insects, a boiler with a fire going under it and the condenser was an old automobile radiator.

I asked, "Dick, do you think we are all right? He said, "Yeah, they are watching us but they don't want any trouble. This thing will be gone tomorrow now that I found it."

Barbara said, "You know, that can't be very sanitary."

21

Family

"The stuff coming out if there is 190 proof so germs are not a problem but the auto radiator is not a real good idea because of the lead in a radiator"

My mother was living with Uncle Ben at that time and one day about dinner time (dinner happens at noon in Tennessee) aunt Jody came to see Little Henry's wife. Barbara was looking sort of confused because aunt Jody was black. She was so old that she had faded to almost white and the first thing that confused Barb was that when they fixed her a plate for dinner she took it out on the back porch to eat it. She and her Husband, Mr. Cason, Had been around and worked for the family for at least 60 years.
Dick died in 1999.

ALICE JEWEL was number two. DOB Sept.5, 1910 Died mid nineties. Alice was the only girl in the bunch and was the pet of the boys and very popular in school making

Family

straight hundreds on her tests.
That was a real hundred.
In those days you learned or
failed. They never heard of grading
on the curve. If you managed to get
out on the curve you can come back
next year and do it again.

When she was about 11 years old she
fell out of the barn loft and hit
her head on something. She was
unconscious for three days and when
she finally came to she was
confused about where she was and
who she was. She never finished
high school and progressively became more disconnected with rea-
lity. She spent several years in a
mental institution and finally they
gave her enough electro shock
treatments she became pretty doc-
ile. They then sent her back to
live with me and mother and mother
alone after I went into the Marine
Corps. By this time aunt Evie and
Aunt Fannie had died and Mom and
Alice moved in with Uncle Ben.
Alice died several years after
mother in the late nineties after
burning up hundreds of family

pictures and keepsakes in the fireplace.

One thing I remember as a kid was a log book from the clipper ship Mary Jane, captain, Jonathan Huddleston sailing out of New Bedford in the spice trade with China. Hand written and salt water stained with entries such as, "Midwatch, wind steady southwest, all standing."

I don't know how uncle Ben got this and I have not been able to find much about it except one man I talked to in Massachusetts, who was actually in the Whaling History Museum, thought he had heard about that ship disappearing on its last voyage. Those clippers were built for fast and carried too much sail. Several of them caught in a weather squall were driven under before they could shorten sail.

CHARLES SAMUEL Born 05/30/1912, Died ??? ?? ????.
Charles Attended David Lipscomb University in Nashville but due to

Family

a disagreement with my father which ended up in fisticuffs behind the barn he didn't finish. Through Senator Gore, Al Gore's father, he got a job as something resembling P.A. to Speaker of the House Sam Rayburn in Washington D.C. He kept that job until the start of the war. I never knew why he left but I think it was a friendly parting because he went to New York and got a job with RCA Communications Cable Division.

There he met Joan Helmers who was secretary to the inventor/developer of television and in due course married her. They had two children,

CHARKES SAMUEL and NICK THURSTON. Her father was Nick Helmers who was Helmers of Simms Helmers Engineering Contractors. A few of their projects were The Key West Bridge in Florida, the Huey Long bridge over the Mississippi in New Orleans, The Carquinez railroad bridge in California and the Blimp hangar at Moffat Field in Mountain View California. Incidentally Charles son, Charle's, wedding reception was held near that hangar many years later.

At the start of the war Simms Helmers were having real problems getting any contracts due to wartime restrictions so Charles said, "You want jobs. I can get you jobs"

He went to Washington on Friday and came back to New York on Monday with the prime contract for the air base Bluie West One in Greenland.

This impressed Nick so much he hired Charles. I am unclear to exactly what his job was but one item marked him for the rest of his life. He went to Minnesota to hire workers who were accustomed to working in cold weather. They had to use steam jennies to melt the permafrost to level the runway. He hired I think 40 men and put them on a ship to Greenland. A German submarine torpedoed the ship with a loss of all hands. Charles refused after that to cross big water.

Family

Walter Beam and Mary Kay gave Charles and Joanne a life estate in four houses on two lots with title to Charles and Nick. Charles and Charles had a disagreement, not unusual in our family, and Charles senior moved off the property.

Charles had picked up some of the beltway arrogance while working in Washington. This stayed with him until his death and was demonstrated when he refused to go to Charles' wedding because he didn't like his selection for wife.
Charles senior cut Charles junior out of his will but this didn't make much difference because Nick and Charles split the proceeds after his death.

BENJAMIN ALBERT, DOB 1/31/1916, Died 03/01/2000.
Ben was raised in Tennessee as the third brother. I can remember him and some neighbor boys playing country music. Ben on Guitar, Joe Jourdan on fiddle and Dave Rucker on banjo. This was in the heyday of the Grand old Opery. With Roy

Family

Acuff, Uncle Dave Macon, Minnie Pearl, The Kentucky Blue Grass Boys all sponsored by Martha White Flour. Guess you would call it a rock session now.

Ben borrowed fifty dollars from uncle Ben and bought a mail order course in fingerprint science. He was working for the Cedars of Lebanon State Park when the war started. Then he got a Job in Chattanooga, Tennessee doing fingerprints for employees of a contractor working on a secret project. This may have been the Oak Ridge uranium refining plant.

Then the draft came along and Ben decided he did not want the army so he talked to a navy recruiter. When the recruiter found out he was a fingerprint specialist he immediately enlisted him in the navy as a seaman first class and sent him to Washington D.C. Never mind boot camp. The navy issued him uniforms and dog tags and sent him to the naval annex near the pentagon. When he reported there the officer in charge told him, "That is your desk, report for work at eight hundred hours tomorrow. You will get subsistence pay. Go and find a place to live."

Ben spent the entire war filing and checking fingerprints in the naval annex. He also had access to personnel records and could find out where your son was and if he was Okay. While at this posting he met and Married Marie Ruble I think after she told him she was pregnant and if he didn't marry her she would jump out the window. They never had any kids.

At the end of the war Ben was hired by the navy as a civilian fingerprint specialist and worked the same job until about 1958 when they moved to California at my suggestion and lived in Burlingame Ca. for three years. Then Ben took a job in Long Beach, Ca. as an auditor with the U.S. Customs service and worked there until he retired around 1978.

Family

Between he and Marie they set a world record for health problems. I think between the two of them they had 23 operations. Marie finally went one too many and died in the late eighties.

Ben moved back to San Mateo in a retirement home and lived until September 2000.

Both Ben and Marie were interred in a crypt at Forest Lawn Cemetary in Los Angeles. Marie insisted on being buried head first to avoid the possibility of being ejected head first in the event of an earthquake. I suppose this came up before she died.

OSTAL JOSEPH, DOB 03/24/1925. (Died 02/07/1927).
Ostal was number five of the litter. He suffered an injury to his forehead which swelled up and refused to heal. They took him to a hospital in Nashville and the doctors decided it was cancer and he should have radium treatments. He started vomiting, all his hair

Family

fell out and he died. Seems like I have heard of symptoms similar to that that somewhere else. Guess they didn't know much about radiation in 1927.

HENRY STONEWALL Born 11/2/1928. Still alive and kicking in '09 Born at 5:00 am in the on a cold and blustery day at home. No doctor. Participated in the milking marathon referred to earlier an soon as I was big enough to squeeze a tit. Remember one year helping to pick cotton. Those cotton bolls are prickly.

Attended Major grammar school which was a country school with three rooms, three teachers and three coal fired stoves. A hand operated pump for well water and two big outhouses. Miss Adeline Baskin was my teacher for the first four years. Miss Ad had a big fat paddle that was a great cure for A.D.D. and a lot of other problems young people seem to have nowadays.

Family

I will comment that living in the country on a farm is a great experience for a young kid. You were expected to help with the chores and anything else that needed doing. It was not unusual for me to take a 22 single action rifle and disappear hunting or just rambling for several hours.

I remember one time Ben and I went hunting and got in a disagreement about something. I went one way and Ben went another. I walked around a corner in the cow path and spotted a razorback hog about 15 yards ahead. My idea was, I will show Ben who is a hunter so I raised the rifle and fired. I saw the bullet lay the skin open right between his eyes. I found out then that of you really want to piss a razorback off, shoot him with a 22 rifle.

I quickly realized that this was something I had not thought of so I dropped the rifle and climbed a tree. The next thing I heard was Ben just doubled over laughing. His

Family

12 gauge shotgun worked better and we had fresh pork for a few days.

My father died in 1940 of Parkinsons disease after a long illness We stayed in the same house for two more years.
My mother and I would hitch the old grey mare to the buggy and travel the 5 or 6 miles to visit uncle Ben, aunt Evie and aunt Fannie at the country general store.

In 1942 we moved to Lebanon. Ben was in the navy and we were supported by the thirty five dollars a month Ben had listed us with the navy as dependents. The rent was fifteen dollars and two dollars would buy more groceries than I could carry. No car, no insurance and no taxes. Life was pretty simple.

I attended Lebanon High School and Worked at a Spur Gas station on weekends. After school I worked for a man who supposedly ran an automobile repair shop. He actually built and maintained bootlegger cars. Wilson county was dry Which means no booze, period. I remember taking a Packard business coupe we had worked on out on the Nashville pike and burying the speedometer needle past 120 miles per hour.

I made several trips up to Knoxville in a Chevrolet pickup to drive interference for a bootlegger run. I would park at a certain place and when I saw the Packard or another car come by I was to follow him. The roads were all two lane and if a police car tried to catch him I was to pull across the road and stop, blocking the police car. Never had to do that but the boot-legger liked me and taught me some driving tricks. Inciden-tally guys like this are the grandfathers of NASCAR.

If you want a thrill sometime try a bootlegger turn. At about 40 miles an hour come off the gas pedal pull the emergency brake full on cut the wheel as far as it will go. When the car has rotated close to 180 degrees release the emergency

Family

brake, jam it into second gear, floor board the gas pedal and straighten the wheel. This will turn a car around in the width of a two lane road. Don't try this on a two lane road until you get the feel for it. I wouldn't try it with any cops around either. Makes them nervous.

Ben had taken me to an airshow at Lebanon when I was about seven and I was hooked although a parachute jumper was killed when his chute didn't open. He hit the ground about 100 yards from the airport. Ben and I were the first ones at the scene. Broke every bone in his body.

When I was 15 I started hanging around the local grass strip airport. They would let me sweep the floor and I graduated up to washing airplanes.

They had a Piper J3 (Cub), a Luscomb Silvaire and an Aeronica. Occasionally either Macmurtry the operator of the airport or his

Family

mechanic Louie Gasser would give me a flying lesson. When I was getting close to 16 I went down to Nashville and paid five dollars for an aviation medical certificate. One day Gasser asked me how old I was. I told him I would be 16 tomorrow. He told me to meet him at the airport at daybreak. I did this and we got into the J3 and made one trip around the pattern. When we landed he got out and said "Don't you break my fucking airplane."

After I landed he entered the solo in my log book, cut off my shirt tail put my name and the date on it and nailed it to the wall of the office. This made me the youngest licensed pilot in the country, for a few minutes.

A few weeks later I took the Cub out on a Saturday afternoon and landed on the cow pasture of my girl friend's father's farm. The parents were in Lebanon for their normal Saturday shopping. I took her for a ride. Everything went fine until I went back to the airport trailing weeds from the landing gear. MacMurtry had some comments.

Soon after I started my senior year at Lebanon High I saw a man standing on the post office steps in a blue uniform with a red stripe on the pants leg and a white cap. I asked him what he was and he said he was in the Marine Corps and did I want to join. I went home and talked to mother and she talked to dick and they agreed. I think they may have known about some of my extracurricular activities with Red Daugherty (pronounced Darty in Tennessee) the bootlegger which helped pay for my aviation activities. I may have been a little inaccurate in telling them my age. Boot camp is another story but the last month of it was rifle range that I loved. At the end of a month's training you fired for record from 200 yards, 300 yards and 500 yards. A perfect score was 340 and the top scorer from the regiment went to the Marine Corps

Family

Rifle Team. I fired 338 and some sob from Kentucky fired 339. From boot camp I went to Camp Lejeune North Carolina for a 6 month course in auto mechanics.

While there another guy named Ellington and I bought a Packard limousine from a funeral parlor for seventy five dollars. WE stood port and starboard duty which meant that each of us had liberty every other weekend. After some night work and acquired government parts. We found that the limo had the same engine as a The Packard ambulance's used by the corps. We had the limo in pretty good condition. We took turns driving five marines from Camp Lejeune to Washington D.C. for a cost of Fifteen dollars each round trip. Leave camp at 5:00 P.M on Friday and get back about 1:00 A.M. Monday.

From there I was transferred to Eva Marine Air Station on Oahu Hawaii. That resulted in several adventures Including getting a 40 foot low bed stuck on the Pali. The one that

Family

sticks in my mind happened near the end of my two year plus tour over there. I had been assigned duty as chauffeur Major General Mitchell who was Commander in Chief of Fleet Marine Force Pacific.(CINCOMFFPAC) He was up for retirement and after a lot of parties and parades I delivered him and his wife to the Matson shipping lines Luriline for a trip around the world.

My first day on duty as a chauffeur did not start as well as I would have liked. The general's aide was a captain and a real nice guy. He explained to me the routine with the general. I had a Buick Roadmaster with white seat covers for a staff car. The car and myself were expected to be immaculate at all times. The car had a garage across the parking lot from the general's office. He had a buzzer on his desk. When it buzzed once he expected to get up, put on his coat and walk out the door. The car was supposed to be there with me holding the door open.

Family

If he buzzed twice I was supposed to run across the parking lot, knock once on his door and report for orders. The first morning I picked him up at his quarters at 0730 hours and delivered him to his office.

At 0900 hours the buzzer sounded twice. I ran across the parking lot, knocked once, entered and said, "Reporting sir." He rattled off a bunch of instructions about what he wanted me to do. "Yes sir." About faced and out the door into the hallway. Suddenly I stopped, toally at a loss. I had no idea what he had said.

The aide was standing there grinning at me. "You don't know what he wants do you?" He explained it to me. Dodged another bullet.

That weekend I drove him and his wife to a party at the Royal Hawaiian hotel in Honolulu. "Pick us up at midnight."

Family

On the dot at midnight I was standing by the car with the door open when he came out of the hotel being led by his wife. He was totally blasted. His wife entered the car first. When he started to get in he hit his forehead on the top of the car and would have fallen. For once I was awake. I grabbed his arm, stuck my knee into his butt and shoved him into the rear seat. About half way back to Eva I heard him say to his wife. "That goddamn kid is all right."

I found that I could buy a fifth of Jim Beam in Honolulu for $2.25 and could sell it on the station for $5.00 and that no one was going to check the trunk of the general's car when I brought it in. The General had black orderly named Timmons so I brought the booze in and Timmons sold it. We split the profits. Being from Tennessee a little bootlegging seemed quite natural.

After I had the general properly installed in his suite on the

Family

Luriline I want to him and told him that I had enjoyed driving for him and I hoped he enjoyed his retirement. He responded "Thank you Corporal. How are you going to get your booze on the station now?"

After I recovered my adam's apple I asked Timmons how he knew about that. Timmons answer was a classic. "He's a general, them m-----f------ knows everthang."

Shortly I was transferred back to Cherry Point North Carolina for discharge so being a dealer I had rigged a flight back to Moffat field on a military R5C on a return flight from Berlin as a part of the western leg of the Berlin air lift. I happened to look at the bulletin board in the barracks and found that I was assigned as brig warden on a troop ship going to Treasure Island.

I set up a watch list from the complement of marines aboard the ship and only slept in about four hour naps the entire trip. I tried to be present each four hours for the watch change. We had twelve prisoners including a crazy Indian who was going back to the states for a dishonorable discharge. He had killed someone in a fight. We also had two guys who were caught in a homosexual act and were also going back for a dishonorable discharge. One night one of them hanged himself with his belt in his cell. No one seemed to be too upset about it. Homosexuals were not popular in the Corps.

When we landed at Treasure Island I delivered the prisoners to the base provost marshal, glad to be rid of them, particularly the Indian.
There is a tradition in the Marines that if you have responsibility for a prisoner and you lose him, you serve his sentence. Don't know what happens if you lose twelve of them.

Two days later I was on a train handcuffed to the Indian delivering him to El Toro Marine Base near Los Angeles. When I turned him over to the Provost marshal at El Toro I told him to be careful with that guy, he is crazy. His response was, "We know how to handle prisoners." A few days later I heard that they had assigned him to a prisoner work detail on the roof of a barracks. He pushed the prisoner chaser off the roof and the fall killed him.

I was sent to Cherry Point North Carolina for discharge in late 1949. The commanding Officer called Ellington and me in to his office and talked about a career in the corps. He offered us the officer candidate course if we would reenlist for another four years. Ninety days later, if we passed the training, we would be commissioned second lieutenants.

I decided I wanted out. Ellington took them up on the offer and was posted to the second division as a platoon commander. He was the first Marine killed in Korea. He was shot the first night on front line guard duty by one of his own men. Nineteen year old kids, scared to death in the dark with loaded weapons are dangerous.

After the Corps I went first home then to Kansas City. Charles got me s job with a wheeler dealer named L. L. Day in Corvallis, Oregon. He had a furnace installing company and also ran an appliance store. I started out as a salesman and after two months decided sales were not for me so I went to work as a furnace installer. I was working piece work and making pretty good money for the time.

One day L.L. called his vice president Jim Richmond in and told him I was making more money than him. This resulted in me leaving the company and going back to Kansas City to live with Charles Joan and the boys. I took a job with Ford Aircraft building B-47 wing assemblies in their Claycomo Plant.

I met a girl named Barbara Cory on a blind date. Four months later we were married in the Nazarene

Family

Church. That was fifty five years ago and she is still around. She sticks pretty good.

About the time Ford lost their cost plus contract and we went to a 40 hour work week rather than seventy six hours. Jim Richmond turned up in Kansas City and hired me to work for Atlas Heating and Ventilating in San Francisco.

I worked for Atlas as a sheet metal worker and later a project foreman for about three years. Jim opened a Peninsula branch of Atlas. I took out a California C-20 contractor license and subcontracted the installation work from Jim.

Very soon I branched out from just Atlas work and built a pretty good reputation for quality work with the General Contractors on the peninsula. I got involved in the equal opportunity movement and got four EOC jobs and lost my shirt on all of them. I should have stood in bed. The company folded in 1969.

Family

I went to work in 1970 for Schlegel Mechanical as an estimator and salesman. Nine months they went broke. Vince Howerton, Richard DiMuzio and me started a new mechanical contracting company called Columbia Mechanical Contractors based in San Francisco.

Richard ran the plumbers and I ran the sheet metal men and did the estimating/bidding. Vince sort of ran us. We built the business up to doing about a million in billing a year and built a good reputation with the building owners in San Francisco.

Richard and I found after we were well into a profitable business that our partner was not Vince but his wife Dorothy who had put up the money. This was not a good situation but we lived with it until Barbra who was working as a bookkeeper for the company was fired by Dorothy and she hired her daughter who needed a job. This was the straw that broke the camels back. Richard and I forced her to buy us out for A hundred thousand each. The day we picked up our checks our wives found us in the Polo Club in Burlingame, celebrating with the checks in our pockets.

I had sold a lot of Carrier air conditioning equipment and won a free trip to Russia. This was the fifth Carrier trip I had won and they were all tour type things but Carrier did a good job.

We got home on a Monday morning about one o'clock and it took a while to get Barbara calmed down when she found that Jon had a new dog. At seven thirty the next morning Russ Will who owned South City Mechanical, a friendly competitor for years, called me saying, "You asshole why aren't you at work here?"

I worked for Russ for about a year. His company was in financial trouble and we managed to sort it out and put him in the black again. About ten years after I left he

Family

went broke again and they found
that his bookkeeper named Sally had
stolen over a million dollars from
the company over the last fifteen
years. Sally went to Jail and Russ
sued his accounting firm.

Barbara and I attended his wedding.
I think it was his fifth, this one
at the Cow Palace. It was a
traditional western wedding in the
arena. Russ had a four horse escort
and the bride was delivered in a
stage coach driven by Monte
Montana. Monte didn't understand
driving a four horse team and
almost tripped up the entire team.

During the ceremony handled by a
judge, since he couldn't find a
preacher who would do it, he said,
"And do you Russel (I cant remember
her name) take this woman to love,
cherish, honor and obey until death
do you part?"

The horse standing directly behind
Russ raised his head and snorted
loudly as horses sometimes do. I
later asked the guy riding that

horse how he made the horse do that. He said I didn't understand horses.

Russ made a serious mistake at the wedding reception in the Cow Palace. He had an open bar and this was he night before the Grand National Horse Show opened. Cowboys can drink an enormous amount of booze.

A long time friend of mine was Herman Bauer of Yano and Bauer Consulting Engineers. Yano died and Herman was not much interested in carrying on the business. I made him a proposal to take over the company in partnership with Richard Ehrenberg and operate it as Design Engineering Services Inc.

One of the first jobs we got was to do the HVAC, plumbing and piping design for a remodel of an IBM building in San Jose including twenty two class of one hundred clean rooms. Richard and I operated the company for the next twenty years. Richard would sell the air

Family

conditioning, plumbing, piping and fire protection design jobs and I got the design work completed.

We usually had about eight people in the company and the last ten years paid ourselves a hundred thousand a year plus goodies.

I sold out to Richard for a hundred thousand in 1999 and said I was retiring. I was seventy and tired of the whole thing. The Orientals had basically taken over the city building inspection departments. They were impossible to deal with. They did not know building construction and refused to listen to anyone. A year later Richard sold the company and when the buyer found out what he had bought closed the operation.

I said I was retired ten years ago. I am now doing consulting for a guy who used to work for us, David Penney, and now has his own consulting firm. He gives me his overflow work and hospital remodel work. Nobody wants hospital

Family

remodel work since there is a government agency called OSHPOD (Office of Statewide Health Planning and Development). I am sure this agency was instituted only to drive consultants crazy.

I have also built three experimental airplanes and only crashed one.

Enough about me.

GRACE VICTORIA HUDDLESTON.
MAIDEN NAME HUDDLESTON.

The family.

The first stories I heard about mothers family were I think my about great grandfather. He was a substantial farmer, Cotton grower and slave holder with large land holdings in middle Tennessee at the time of the civil war.

He went to a slave auction in Nashville before the war and bought two black girls about 6 years old. They did not speak English and none

Family

of the slaves spoke their language. No one realized it but they were starving. They unloaded them from the wagon and left them in the back yard where here were several cherry trees with the fruit was just ripening. They ate a lot of the cherries including the pits and both of them died. The family has been hesitant to admit it but the first two graves in the family graveyard are those two girls.

At the end of the Civil War he went to the slaves and told them they were free now and could go anywhere they wanted. They had no idea of where to go or what to do so they just stayed. The economy was in a total collapse condition and there was no market for anything the farmers could produce. He gradually sold off parts of his property to keep some food and basic necessities for the family and the slaves who worked as they had before emancipation. Over the years the slaves gradually went their own ways although many of their descendents still live in the area and

Family

some of them assumed the Huddleston name.

One of his sons was Lafayette Huddleston who married Mary Elizabeth Burke. During the battle of Fall River in the civil war Mary sat on her front porch and listened to the cannon fire while her husband fought in the battle.

One of Lafayette's brothers rode with Carlsons Raiders. When the war ended they were up in Indiana and Carlson called them all together and said, "Boys, the war is over, We lost. You all can go on home now." That was their discharge from the confederate army.

He and some other men had horses, this was a requirement of being a raider, and they started to Tennessee. There was no food and no one they met would admit having anything to eat. At one point they caught a snake and fried him in his cast iron skillet. He carried the skillet tied to his saddle and

Family

every time it rattled against his
rifle he would get sick. When they
got a couple of miles from home
they stopped at Fall Creek to water
the horses. The skillet rattled
against the rifle when the horse
bent down to drink. He cut the rope
and the skillet disappeared into
the creek.

LaFayette and Mary had eight
children who lived. Benjamin
Napoleon. Talmage, George, Oscar,
Bud, Mary Elizabeth (aka Jake),
Fannie, Evie and Grace Victoria. An
interesting note about grandmother
Mary, She died at age 94 still
smoking a corncob pipe with Kill-
deer tobacco and could read a
newspaper by moonlight without
glasses.

OSCAR W. Born June 6, 1868 — Died
March 16, 1943. Married Willie
Vaughter. When I knew him he lived
in Lebanon and apparently his main
source of income was serving on
juries. Aunt Willie would come to
visit and entertain us by patting

Family

her foot on the floor and singing humorous songs. Bear in mind there was no radio or television and the only music you heard was what you or someone made. Some of the richer people had a wind up gramaphone with a big speaker. The sound quality was not very good and something was always going wrong with them. They had three children, Harley, Amy and Grady.

CARLOS C. — Born — Feb. 18, 1870 — Died Jan. 6, 1948.
Commonly called Bud. Married Elizabeth Cluck — One child, died in infancy.
Uncle Bud was for years elected justice of the peace. In Tennessee a J.P could perform marriages, arbitrate civil disagreements, notarize documents and other duties. He also performed the census every four years.

He was also partial to the demon rum on occasion. Once in a while he would go down to Nashville and after three or four days Uncle Ben and Uncle Tal would go down there and find him drunk in the gutter, or elsewhere. They would bring him home and go get Doctor Lee. The good doctor would knock him out with laudanum, the polite name for opium, for a couple of days. Then he was good for another two or three months. He had a disease they called palsy which caused uncontrolled tremor of the hands. He had a beautiful brace of Colt 44/40 revolvers and when he sighted them at something the hands were as steady as a rock. The revolvers disappeared when he died.

EVALINE(Aunt Evie) Born Apr. 25, 1872 — Died Dec.19, 1950.
She never married and lived in the family house all her life. She was a rabid crossword puzzle worker and could hardly wait for the Nashville Banner to be delivered by the mail man. She was also very active in running the general store. She never learned to drive but later in life she bought a big boxy old Essex sedan. She may have ridden in it two or three times. She was very addicted to snuff.

Family

FRANCIS (Aunt Fannie) Born Jan.14, 1874 — Died Nov. 4, 1940.
She never married and lived in the family house all her life. Aunt Fannie was a very nice, gentle woman who panicked when some conflict arose. She was the official cook in the later years of her life at the family home.

GEORGE A. Born Feb. 1, 1876 — Died Dec. 14, 1957.
Married Annie Preston - Five Children - Hoyt, William L., Geraldine, Rosa L. and Mary. Hoyt became a Southern Baptist Preacher and served in WW-2 as a chaplain in Patton's Third Army.

Mary (Aunt Jake ?) Born Feb 2, 1878 — Died Apr. 4, 1964.
Married Albert W. Shingleton — No children. Uncle Al was a school teacher for years and a farmer. He named his farm Evergreen. He was something of an inventor. He had a Ford Model A roadster and he rigged it to use water injection about eighty years before it became

normal usage in some performance engines. When I told him that I was taking flying lessons his advice was to fly very low and slow. He though that was god's area.

BERTIE Born 1880 — Died 1888

BENJAMIN NAPOLEON - Born 1883 - Died February 2, 1965 never married. He took over the remains of the family farm, in a loose partnership with Evie and Fannie on Norene road and Mary lived with them until she died.

Some time in the 1890's Benjamin started a peddling route in partnership with Talmage in the local countryside. This was later developed into a country general store. The store building still exists at this location. Uncle Ben was the favorite of all Walter and Grace's children and we all spent a lot of time at their house and hanging around the country store. Dick lived with then for several years and had a business of shoeing

Family

horses until he got a job at the Cedar Forest.

I stayed there a lot in the summer and Uncle Ben taught me to shoot with a 22 rifle. The front porch of the store faced a gravel road and across the road were some large flat limestone rocks. Peddlers would come by (wholesale reps.) and Uncle Ben would con them into shooting the rifle at a target across the road. The bet was a Coca Cola. He would have me set up an empty 22 shell casing on the flat rock about 50 feet away. The peddler would shoot first and usually miss. The peddler would say something like, "All right Mr. Ben, let's see if you can hit it."

His answer was, "I just let the boy do the light shooting." and hand me the rifle. I never missed. The reason was that uncle Ben showed me how to hit the rock about six to eight inches in front of the shell casing. The soft lead bullet would fragment and scatter blowing the shell case away if I hit anywhere close to the target point. Uncle Ben got a smug look on his face and enjoyed his coke.

Uncle Ben was blind in one eye and could bark a squirrel in a tree at forty or fifty feet. For you city slickers, barking a squirrel is to catch him lying on a tree limb and hit the bark of the limb under him thereby knocking him off the tree without damaging the meat. Squirrel, rabbit, duck, various other birds and frog legs were a part of our regular diet.

We didn't have electricity then and the ice man came once a week and delivered 100 pounds of ice to keep the cokes and Knee Highs cold. I remember he had the first radio in the area operated on a car battery. The boxing match between Joe Lewis and Max Schmelling drew a crowd of about fifteen men who came to listen on the radio. This was the only radio in the area. They were all disgusted when Lewis finished the match in one minute and thirty

Family

six seconds. Ben had a stroke and died a year later at age eighty two, leaving the farm to my mother. The store had closed by that time.

GRACE VICTORIA - Born August 11,1885 — Died Mar. 23, 1975. Married Walter Albert Huddleston — My mother was a woman of strong character. She was born in a dog-trot cabin in a backwoods part of Tennessee just when the state was beginning to recover from the devastating effect of the civil war. She married Walter Huddleston and they had a family as described in this memoir. She lived through a start as a poor family, married Walter and lived through about 18 years of plenty of money and a good stable family. Then the economic crash and depression came along which erased all their assets. Walter worked for the WPA until he contracted Parkinsons disease. We lived pretty much on charity by relatives for four years Until Walter died in 1940. Mother finally had a stable income, first from Ben's navy allotment and later from

Family

my allotment. When Evie and Fannie died she and Alice moved in with Uncle Ben. This gave her a stable home and environment. She almost made 90 years old. One day she said, "I'm a little tired, think I'll lay down for a few minutes." An hour later Alice went in to ask her something and she was dead.

TALMAGE G. Born in 1887 — Died February 4, 1974.
Tal married Hanna Bell (last name unknown) and they had no children. He was a farmer and a partner with Ben in the peddling route, the store operation and several farms they bought and sold. They would buy a farm from some one who could not make a living on it because the land had been overworked so badly. The per acre production was not adequate to offset the cost of production. They would plant the entire tillable acreage in clover, wait until it matured and plough it under. The next year they would plant corn and grow a bumper crop. Then sell or trade the farm. They seemed to understand the effect of

nitrogen fixing but I doubt if they even knew what nitrogen was.

Nobody seemed to like Hannah Bell much but she was family and you dealt with what you had. After Tal died she sold the farm and moved to Lebanon. Running water, sewer, electricity and even air conditioning. Don't know if and when she died.

THE NEXT GENERATION

BARBARA and HENRY had three children,

VICTORIA JO — Born 6/22/57 — Died, Not yet.
Vicki attended Fiesta Gardens School, San Mateo Park School and San Mateo High school. Played clarinet in the high school marching band and marched at the 1972 inauguration of president Nixon.

Vicki graduated from Point Loma college in San Diego With a degree in child psychology. She met a guy named Rickie Bland. They were married in San Mateo and had four

Family

children Jamie, Patrick, Ryan and Kristen. They lived in Fresno for a while, then San Mateo. Rick was selling electrical supplies until got ordained as a minister in the Christian Missionary Alliance Church. He supposedly was cured at a prayer meeting of Hodgkins disease. This brought him to the attention of the church management. They moved the family to Colorado Springs and put him in as minister to the local Church. They also sent him on a mission to the Philippines to spread the word. They discovered that the Hodgkins disease cure was a lie and that he had embezzled church funds by forging one of the deacons signature. Vicki filed for divorce.

Vicki was hired by the Christian Missionary Alliance headquarters in Colorado Springs and supported her family.

She later met a man named Kevin Khoury and they were married October 7, 2000. Interesting to note that Barbara's maiden name was

Family

Cory. Guess the difference is between English and Lebanese family origins. At any rate, this time she found a winner from a very good family in Oklahoma City. They Later moved to Oklahoma City. Kevin is currently acting as the supervisor of setting up a small hospital in Oklahoma City. Vicki's primary interest now is baby sitting her new grandson Named Liam Kai Cory and singing in the Canterbury Chorus in Oklahoma City.

JAMIE - Born May 16, 1981 — Jamie is a beautiful girl. They lived in Colorado Springs and when she was sixteen she went to a high school campfire with a bunch of students. One boy was shooting his friends in the butt with a pellet gun. He missed her boyfriend and hit her in the corner of her eye. The pellet went through her sinus cavity and through her brain stopping about one half inch from the back of her skull. Amazingly enough she lived. There were several operations to try to repair the damage but she has lost most of her sense of taste and smell. She will probably be on medication for the rest of her life for epileptic seizures as a result of all this. She has met and married David Torchin on Sept. 2, 2006 and now lives in Oklahoma City. David is a sheet metal worker and since that is the way I started out he I think he was a good selection.

PATRICK - Born October 11 1983 — Patrick graduated from High school in Colorado Springs and had most of the problems that young men experience. Pat worked for a while for a building contractor and decided he could do a better job than these turkeys. He is now working as a bartender and going to college to be an architect. He married Marye Elizabeth Williams May 10, 2008 and they have a Son Liam Kai who is a great, great grand son.

RYAN Born - May 9, 1986. — Ryan graduated from high school in a school somewhere in New England. He held several jobs one of which looked pretty good, installing

Family

transponders in commercial trucks, until the depression got them. He found a chain of specialty Gas station / food and everything stores Ryan is now manager of a new one in Oklahoma City. Ryan is not married --- yet.

KRISTEN — Born Jan.21, 1990 — Kristen is the kid of the litter. She graduated from high school in Oklahoma City and now is attending the University of Oklahoma and will be a sophomore this fall. She seems to always have a serious boy friend but no commitments yet. That I know of. She is interested in fashion design and is considering a school in San Francisco

JONATNAN HENRY — Born Oct.19, 1959 — Died, Not yet.

This makes Jon the ninth Henry in our line of Huddlestons.
Jon attended Fiesta Gardens School, San Mateo Park School, and San Mateo High school.

Family

While still in high school Jon had a pickup truck and started hauling garbage for people in the neighborhood. Jon has gone through a plethora of trucks and he has learned how to keep them running. He and a friend made a trip to Washington after mount St. Helens erupted to collect some volcanic dust. It stayed in our garage for several years until I finally dumped it. After high school he had a trip to Europe, a year or so at the family farm in Tennessee, a hitch as a cab driver and a long haul driver for DHL shippers.

The hauling business has survived all these events and presently he has a crew and hauls about anything to anywhere and specializes in demolition work. He will tear your house down and haul it away, if you pay him enough.

Jon had a session with alcohol and is now has been a supporting member of Alcoholics Anonymous for over 20 years. He is also a visiting speaker at many of their regular meet-

Family

ings. AA seems to be the only organization of its type that really works on a sustained basis. I think that is at least partly due to the fact that under their bylaws the association is not allowed to own anything, including cash.

He met a delightful woman at an AA meeting and married her. Patricia (Pat) nee Wells and they live in San Mateo.

He has a daughter Michelle Haltenhof, Her mother is Dale Haltenhof. She is now seventeen years old. He and Pat have another child, Katherine (Katie) who is eleven.

Jon claims he is as rascally as any of the Huddlestons including Wild Jack. He also claims to be a world traveler having been in 49 states and 15 countries. Dick carried a ten dollar confederate in his wallet until he died. Jon now carries one.

MICHELLE Born Feb. 27, 1992. Now has a drivers License. Look Out!! —

Family

She is working this summer for an ice cream store named Cold Stone. I am presently up two pounds in weight. She is a senior and getting close to deciding what her career will be but young kids don't feel the pressure we older people do.

KATHERINE MARIE(KATIE) Born June 13, 1998. She is in the sixth grade and heavily into Ballet training. One time on vacation Jon was sitting on the edge of a creek with his feet on a rock. Katie very calmly said, "Dad look between your feet." There was a snake crawling by. Jon did a pretty good imitation of a space shuttle lift off.

NANCY ANN — Born 2/2/62 — Died, Not yet.

NANCY attended Fiesta Gardens School, San Mateo Park School, and San Mateo High school. She attended Southern Oregon State College and Hunter College in New York City.

Family

When Nancy was almost sixteen she came to me and said, "Jon got a truck at sixteen, Vicki got a Mustang at sixteen. What do I get?"

I told her I thought it would be fun to rebuild an old English sports car if we could find one. I went to work the next morning and that afternoon she called me and said, "Dad, I found the car." We rebuilt an Austin Healy and she drove it while she was at Oregon State. Somewhere along the line she stripped the second gear out of the transmission and I refused to fix it. She sold it and bought a Triumph GT6B in pretty sick condition so we rebuilt it.

She moved to New York to go to school at Hunter College and try out to be an actress. The school didn't work out but she lived in a loft in Soho and made a living at various jobs while she tried out for acting. Got several parts in off/off Broadway but never hit the big time.

Family

She and a friend came out to California and rebuilt our kitchen. She lived in San Francisco for about a year then moved to Boston with the intention of starting a home delivery pet supply company.

While waiting to get that started she met a woman who asked her if she knew anything about show business. She got hired as a gofer on a television commercial producer crew. She now works freelance in Hollywood as a producer /production manager for television commercials. She sits around for two or three weeks then when she gets a job it's 6:00 am until 10:00 pm or later until they wrap.

She Lived near a woman named Elizabeth Emanuel who had worked in the movie industry for over 50 years and her assumed niece Tanya Frank. Tanya has two boys Zack, twenty and Dale, twenty one. Both boys are in college. The older woman died and the two girls inherited a very nice house in Hollywood that had had no maintenance in 20 years. They are working on it.

CHARLES and JOAN had two children Nick and Charles — twins.

CHARLES (Chuck) Attended high school in Palo Alto California. and college in San Jose, graduating with a degree in philosophy. He then took a job with Bekins Van Lines and worked for them twenty five years.

During that time he met and married Jana LaLanne. The wedding reception the officers club at Moffat Field near the blimp hangar in Mountain View, Ca. that his grandfather Nick Helmers had built in the nineteen thirties. They had one child, Heather.

Jana was some kind of relative to Jack LaLanne the physical fitness guru in the fifties. She also developed into channeling and I don't pretend to understand that.

Family

Jana was some kind of relative to Jack LaLanne the physical fitness guru in the fifties.

When they broke the Union Charles quit Bekins, and they moved to Hawaii. They bought and remodeled a house in Kaneohe. Heather graduated from Punahou. Jana took up channeling and Chuck met a traveling Guru and decided he was a Hindhu. I don't pretend to understand either one.

Jana's channeling took them to Sweden. It was a rough trip and they came back to Hawaii, sold their home in Aptos, and divorced. Jana returned to Sweden and Chuck went to India for 6 months of Ashram life then swung back through Hawaii and, not being one to give up easily, went back to Sweden after Jana. It didn't work out, Chuck met someone else and stayed in Sweden for ten years. Jana married someone else. Since he was technically an illegal alien, he got under the table work, at a New Age farm, to support himself.

Family

He came back to the U.S. looking to live in his Guru's Ashram. When that wasn't possible, he came back to California and bought a van, which he still has, and wandered Around the Northwest for about a year then took a job with Dede, the wife of Walter Beam, his in-law uncle. She is operating a rest home for Alzheimer patients in Santa Cruz and Chuck is good at dealing with them on outings etc.

We enjoy heckling each other. I think he is an unembarrassed liberal and he thinks I am somwhere to the right of Atilla The Hun. I think we sort of like each other which is nice for relatives.

NICK (not Nicholas) Attended high school in Palo Alto California. He then attended the University of California at Berkley and got a degree in oceanography. He also met and married Mary _____ at a wedding where only people under thirty five were invited. This was in the days of college students protesting even if they didn't know anything about whatever in hell they were protesting. Not sure much has changed there.

They moved to Taos New Mexico and Nick taught math in a high school. While they were there they had one child Matthew. Did not take Nick long to decide that teaching was not for him. He got a divorce and moved to Washington State.

In Washington he met and married a wonderful woman named Pamela Stewart who was a librarian at the local university. She had an offer of a job as head librarian at the University of Hawaii and they moved to Honolulu.

There Nick entered the university and got a degree in architecture. He is now a practicing architect in Hawaii. Matthew lived with them through high school until he went to college in New England. Pamela retired from the university and became a partner in a chain of very successful hobby supply stores in

Family

the islands. She sold her interest in the stores and they travel all over the world between Nick's architectural jobs. They have a delightful home on Wilhelmina Rise in Honolulu. That is if walking on the sidewalk in front of the house at night and crushing cockroaches under your shoes doesn't bother you. I do not recommend barefoot night strolls.

AND THE NEXT GENERATION.

HEATHER, Born July 29, 1968 Charles and Jana's daughter. Graduated from high school in Hawaii and basically worked her way through the university system until she got a doctorate in literature and now is a tenured professor a the Indiana University in Indiana, Pennsylvania. Don't ask me about that name combination.

Shortly after hooding she married Mike Powers and accepted the position in Pennsylvania. They have two children, Henry America, born August 15, 2002 making him the tenth Henry in the blood line but the last name is Powers. Luchia Serenity Born March 6, 2006. Both kids are healthy and thriving in Pennsylvania — if that is possible.

Mike is some kind of computer guru and for a while I think he worked for NSA. I believe he now works for the University running their web site. I hear rumors occasionally about them moving to California. It would probably be tough to leave tenure.

MATTHEW Born Sept. 11, 1968. Son of Nick and Mary. After the divorce Matthew lived with Nick and Pamela in Honolulu. Graduated from Punahou High school. Spent some time with a family in China and speaks Chinese. Graduated from Bates college with a degree in English Literature. Won a Watson scholarship. Used the money to study the digiredoo with the aborigines in Australia. I don't know about the spelling but the thing is a musical instrument. I think.

Family

He wandered around the South
Pacific for a while then came back
to the states got married to
Jennifer Parmelee and entered
medical school. Served his inte-
rnship at The University of California Medical School in San
Francisco.

He is now practicing medicine in
Massachusetts (why do they always
call it practicing, don't they know
how before they start on people? He
and Jen own a farm a farm that has
been in Jen's family for gener-
ations. They have two children
Clarity Jane Born Oct. 18, 1997 and
Hanna born April 25, 2001. My son
Jon has visited them and I think
they are jokers. The girls stole
his polka dot under shorts and ran
them up a flagpole.

LIAM KAI Born Nov. 5, 2008. Son of
Patrick and Mary. Last of the
Huddleston blood line, for a while.
Liam's mother Marye Elizabeth is
half Chinese so Liam is one quarter
Chinese.

Family

THE CORY LINE

HAROLD MARTIN CORY — Born Nov. 20,1905—Died Sept. 30, 1987. Harold was born in Scammon, Kansas and attended school in El Reno, Oklahoma. He worked for the Rock Island Railroad for forty four years. He married Marion Bruce and they had three children, Barbara Jo, Donald Bruce, And Wilma Sue. They were later divorced and Harold married Mildred Swenson. Mildred died after about twelve years. Harold then married Rosa Hernandez who was his wife until he died in 1987. They lived in Weslaco, Texas.

MARION BRUCE CORY — Born July 20,1907 - Died May 20, 1969. Harold and Marion lived first in El Reno then he was transferred to Kansas City, Missouri by the Rock Island. Marion was a wonderful grandmother for our kids until and lived with us for about the last year of her life. She was proud of the fact that during World War Two she worked for Pratt and Whitney making aircraft engines.

I remember one time I took Barbara on a surprise trip to Los Angeles for dinner with Bill and Lola Martin. She thought we were going to San Francisco and just before we left the house I told Marion where we were going. She looked kind of shocked and said, "Well I wish you had told me sooner. What if something happens?"

SUE NOBRIGA Nee Walker, nee Doyle, Nee CORY. Barbara's sister. Born Sept. 11 1935. Three Children, Randy Walker —, Jennifer Doyle, Joseph Doyle — born xxx xx xxxx. Sue is presently married to Dave Nobriga Born 1919. For years Sue operated a child care facility until health problems caused her to stop. They presently live in San Mateo, Ca.

RANDY WALKER - Born Jan. 13 1956. Randy lived with his mother after her divorce and her marriage to Joe

Family

Doyle. He graduated from high school in Millbrae. California. He worked in law enforcement at several jurisdictions around the state and also as a truck inspector for an insurance company. He married Laura Sharp and they had one child, Jeremiah.

He then married Donya GOOD. They have three children, Rachel, Rebecca and Jebediah and presently live in Fresno California where he is pursuing a career in auto racing and Donya is a registered nurse.

JENNIFER DOYLE - Born April 30 1971. Jennifer lived with her mother until her marriage to Michael Lorton. They had one child, David Michael. They then got a divorce and shared custody of the child.

Jennifer then married Mark Semeit. They have three children, Tyler, Mark's child by a previous marriage, Shane and Travis. Now living in Woodland, California near Sacramento.

Family

Joseph Doyle — Born Feb. 18 1968. Married Gilda Lezama They had two children, Jacob and Daniella. After a divorce they have limited shared custody. There is another child named Kirra, Daughter of Jamie Green. Joseph presently resides in Hayward, California.

DONALD BRUCE CORY — Born Nov. 6, 1931. Don Graduated at Paseo high school in Kansas City, Missouri. He served aboard the USS Helena during the Korean war. While in the navy he met Angela June Kronmiller in Los Angeles and they were married April 29, 1955. They had three children, Donna Marie, Brenda Jeanine and Christopher Bruce.

Don worked for several years as truck driver finally working for th Arco refining company in Long beach California. Don was promoted to supe rintendent of transportation wit about one hundred Freightliners in hi division and worked that job until hi retirement.

Family

Don and I have always been good friends but occasionally I think I irritated him. I remember one day I started to work in San Francisco and the freeway was completely blocked by an Arco Tanker on fire in front of the airport. When I finally got to the office I called Don and complained about his truck making me late for work. I heard him using bad language before he slammed the phone down. Guess he was a little "otherwise occupied".

BRENDA JEANNINE — Born May 5, 1958. Graduated from high school in Sylmar, California. Brenda married Charles Pore and they had two children, Heide and Holly. Brenda got custody of the girls after the divorce and supported them by working in the accounting division at Arco. She later moved to Houston and worked for the accounting firm that was the accountants that did work for Imron before they went broke big time.

DONNA LORRAINE — Born Sept. 8, 1960. Graduated from high school in

Family

Sylmar, California and attended. She married Timothy Chaney who has worked for General Motors for many years. They had two Children Adam and Zachary. Tim likes to buy and sell houses, they currently live in Fort Wayne, Indiana where they both work for G.M.

CHRISTOPHER — Born — Dec. 28, 1970. Graduated from high school in Sylmar, California. Later attended College of the Canyons and got an A.A. Degree in Computer Electronics and presently works for a telephone communications company. He married Stacy Wight who had a daughter Dannielle and they had another child, Nathaniel. Chris liked motorcycle racing until he broke a leg. Now he likes dune buggies. They now live in Acton California.

THE NEXT GENERATION.

HEIDE — Born Nov. 6, 1979. Graduated from High school in Palmdale, California. Served in the U.S. Airforce with a hitch in the Kuwait area and a tour on The

Family

Azores islands. She met Will Thornsbury and they were married on April 24, 2004. They now have two Children, Cannan and Gavin and live in Fredricksburg, Virginia.

HOLLY — Born Jan. 1, 1981. Graduated from High school in Palmdale, California. Moved with her mother to Houston, Texas. She married Asher Light June 30, 2005 He is currently in residency for doctor training. They have one child named Sterling Light.

I'm tired of the whole thing and probably so are you.

END